TWO DAYS "LOST" IN

AMSTERDAM

GONE WITHOUT A TRACE: 48 HOURS IN THE FOG

JOOLS JONES

BlueRose ONE
Stories Matter

BLUEROSE PUBLISHERS UK Ltd.
London

This book is primarily published and distributed in Great Britain and is also available in other global marketplaces.

BlueRose ONE
Stories Matter

ISBN: 978-93-7139-582-3

Designed and distributed by **BlueRoseONE.com** with global reach. Printing and fulfilment are managed through international distribution networks, ensuring availability based on order locations.

For publishing inquiries, visit **www.BlueRoseONE.com**

BlueRose Publishers UK Ltd,
Unit 3, 6-7 St Mary at Hill, London

+44 7386286323

First Edition: July 2025

In memory of my great friend,

Andrew Fitton. Gone, but never forgotten.

About the Author

I live a quiet life in rural Cheshire with my rescue dog, Max. This is my second publication after "Tails of the Unexcepted" under the name William Turner, a book about my life working with dogs. I previously had a doggie day care, boarding, walking, training and grooming business.

Now retired my days are filled with outdoor adventures alongside Max, pursuing writing, piano lessons (still a work in progress!), performing on stage in my local theatre, and occasional minor television roles in commercials and films.

Contents

Introduction

This is based on a true story that took place over three decades ago. When I say two days "lost" in Amsterdam, I don't mean I was wondering around unable to find my hotel, but rather I had almost two days of total and complete memory loss. Absolutely no recollection of what happened to me between Friday afternoon and Sunday morning.... zero, nada, nothing at all, a total blank in my memory banks.

I was living in London at the time where I started my career working in the travel industry. I was 23 years old. One of the great perks of working in this sector certainly wasn't the pay, but the opportunity to go and visit many places, cities and countries. Travelling was, and still is, something I love to do. I have been to over 40 counties now and still have a long "bucket" list of paces I haven't yet been to.

I initially worked for a tour operator and then moved into business travel for a large conglomerate. We were frequently awarded free flights with airlines we sold a lot of tickets for, and free hotel nights with groups that we used as preferred suppliers.

So, on this occasion I had a free business class ticket with KLM, the Dutch airline, and two free nights at a Marriott

Hotel. Four other colleagues from different London offices had also been rewarded the same perk and the obvious choice was to fly direct from Heathrow to Amsterdam. I didn't know the others, in fact none of us knew each other and so via emails we quickly agreed on the location, it was just a question of finding at date when we were all free.

And so, it was done, we each booked a Friday off work, the flights and hotel, then simply arranged to meet at the KLM check in desk at the allocated time. We were to leave on a Friday morning and return Sunday afternoon.

Amsterdam

I had been to Amsterdam once before, and several times since later in life, and really like the place. It's a great city to visit if you haven't been I would highly recommend it.

Yes, it's a bit of a tourist trap for stag and hen weekends with the coffee bar culture (which is exactly why I went on this occasion) and red-light district. It has several world-famous nightclubs and is known for the festivals and liberal openness. But it has so much more to offer.

Firstly, it's Holland capital city with a population of close to a million, plus a further 4 million in the urban and metropolitan areas, and is consequently a very busy place and is a multicultural destination with over 180 different nationalities living there. It is also one of Europe's financial hubs and has one of the oldest stock exchanges in the world with the fifth largest port in Europe.

It has a wide artistic heritage and houses many museums, including the Van Gogh Museum which has a wide range to art from Rembrandt to modern art at the Stedeliik. The 17th century architecture from The Golden Age in itself is well worth seeing. It has narrow canal houses from that era which were apparently build tall and narrow to reduce the high cost of ground taxes at that time.

The spectacular elaborate canal system stemming from the river Amstel, which gives it the nick-name of the "Venice of The North". A great place to hire a bike to cycle around and swallow up the diverse history and heritage, or jump on the tram system with sixteen different routes to take.

If you don't try to Stroopwafels, which are thin waffles filled with caramel syrup, and Bitterballen, which are fried meat balls, then you have missed a major treat.

Check In

We all met up at the check in desk at Heathrow as arranged and were bound for Schiphol airport. Introductions were made and we headed for an overpriced beer after passing through security.

The others were two other guys, whose names I honestly can't remember so we will call them Steve and Tom. The other two were girls, one called Charlotte and the other Vanessa. We were all of a similar age and they all seemed very friendly and excited about the weekend ahead.

I rather took an immediate shine to Vanessa and hoped to get to know her better over the weekend, much better! She was petit with a lovely smile, cute butt and shoulder length dark hair with an ample chest that strained against her blouse with each breath, and sparkling dark eyes. At the time in my life, I was a bit of a ladies' man, or at least I liked to think so. I was hopeful.

We all chatted over a drink and on the plane, getting to know each other, then on landing and collecting our luggage we took the train into town and could walk to the hotel from there.

and so chatted with Tom and Steve and a little with Charlotte who was clearly the quietist of the group. Burgers and chips arrived and were devoured in almost silence (I always found food got in the way of conversation) and then a third round was ordered by Steve and the chat accelerated in a more open way, now that everyone was beginning to relax and the beer was taking effect. So, I suggested that if anyone wanted to partake in a spliff that I would go and buy a couple. Everyone nodded agreement and grinned, Charlotte suggesting that the weakest type would be better. Fair enough I thought, it might be the first time for her. I of course acted as if I were a seasoned pro in such matters and told them to leave it with me.

There was a separate counter next to the bar, with an equally huge hairy guy sat behind it, smoking a spliff that was beautifully constructed and was massive. A "Camberwell Carrot" I laughed to myself, from the film Withnail and I. There was a menu crudely sellotaped to the desk. The menu had brief descriptions of the different types of weed and strengths of them, as you could purchase one spliff at a time rather than having to buy an eighth or quarter at a time. Only in Amsterdam I though, God I loved this place. I ordered just two spliffs of the weakest variety and headed back to the table.

I handed one to Tom and pulled out my Zippo to light the other, inhaling deeply before passing it to Vanessa. I was probably trying a little too hard to look "cool" but hoped it went unnoticed.

The afternoon went by quickly and evening came, the beers continued to flow (although the girls were slipping behind in the rounds and were sensibly pacing themselves) and more spliffs were smoked. We were all laughing and joking, and now all sense of discretion had long since gone. Stories were exchanged and the conversation was now totally nonchalant, without any concern or embarrassment. Even Charlotte was now looking totally relaxed. I found myself sitting closer to Vanessa who was now frequently resting her hand on my arm whilst laughing at my stories. She at one point laughed into my shoulder and I could feel her hair tickling my ear.

I was beginning to become aroused and didn't bother trying to hide it from her. In fact, the opposite. I looked into her eyes and lowered my gaze to my lap, I looked up at her again and her eyes had followed mine and she was now staring at my groin, she looked back up at me and giggled more, this time with a slight blush in her checks and she lent in and softly kissed my neck just below my ear. Now I could feel her breath in my ear and it felt good. She had indicated that she had a boyfriend but was bored of him and I strongly emphasised that I was very single.

That, unfortunately, was about the last thing I remembered.

Rude Awakening

Bang, bang, bang. Shouting.

"Julian, are you there?"

Bang, bang, bang.

"Hello, are you there?"

It was Vanessa. I began to stir from what must have been a deep sleep. I was lying on a bed, still fully clothed, and took a while to register where on earth I was. It was my hotel room, with my hand luggage lying on the floor, bag unzipped but nothing removed. I rubbed my eyes and groaned.

"Just a minute" I shouted back.

I stood up uneasily, legs wobbling and with a mouth that felt like the bottom of a bird cage. I opened the door, blinking at the light.

"Oh, thank God, What the hell happened to you?"

"Err, I'm not sure, is everything ok?"

"No, we have to go. We need to get the train in 20 mins to the airport"

"Airport?" I enquired, covering my mouth with my hand. I could smell my own breath and it wasn't good. "What for?"

"To get our flight of course".

"Flight? But we haven't got to go now. Has something happened?"

She looked worried. "It's Sunday, we have to get going. You've been missing since Friday. We've been so worried but no-one had your number!"

"Sunday? Very funny! What happened last night? It's all a bit hazy."

She held out her phone to show me the display. "It's Sunday, what are you talking about? Come on, get ready, we have to leave in 15 minutes. We're all waiting in the lobby" With that she turned and left me standing there.

I was so confused. I grabbed and checked my own phone, thinking this was a wind up. It read 10.38, Sunday. What the fuck? I staggered slightly as I went into the bathroom, gathering my wash bag from the open case on the way, I quickly brushed my teeth, sprayed on some deodorant and changed tops. I had no time to think. Zipped up my bag and managed to remember to check for my passport and rushed out of the room, I punched the elevator button to head to the lobby. The lift door opened and the others were there waiting, all staring at me. I was sweating and felt so confused that I still hadn't had time to realise how ill I was feeling too.

They all gathered around me and were firing questions to which I had no answers. I simply couldn't understand that it was Sunday.

"Where have you been?" "What happened to you?" "We've been so worried" "We were going to phone the police" "No-one has seen you since Friday evening" "Are you alright?" "You look terrible" ….and so on.

"Err" I said, rubbing my bloodshot eyes and trying desperately to remember anything, "I don't know, I can't seem to remember anything"

"Nothing at all since Friday?" Vanessa screeched.

"No, I don't think so. When did you last see me?"

"We've not seen you since Friday night," said Tom. "You just disappeared. We checked your room yesterday morning to come and get you for some sightseeing but you weren't in. I assumed you had met some girl and spent the night with her. Then there was still no sign of you when we got back to the hotel yesterday afternoon."

"Err" I said again. "So, none of you have seen me all day yesterday?" I enquired, now feeling like death warmed up and added to that, extremely embarrassed. "I honestly can't remember anything at the moment."

Steve interjected "The last I saw of you is you were chatting outside The Grasshopper to some guy. You had been really hammering the beers and spliffs, we couldn't keep up with you"

I coughed and said nothing. Charlotte was staring at me from behind the others. In fact, they were all staring at me. The girls had worried looks and Steve and Tom were smirking at me.

"It's not funny" I pleaded. "I don't know what happened. I can't believe it's Sunday. I have just lost two days of my life!!"

Steve started laughing, so much that tears were coming out of the corner of his eyes. "You mad bastard!"

Vanessa walked up to me and lightly slapped me on the chest. "You bloody idiot, I was really worried. Well at least you are ok anyway. Now we need to get going"

The journey home was uncomfortable. I continued to sweat and even started shaking a little. I tried to sleep on the train and flight with no luck. The others chatted about what they had been up to over the weekend and I just listened, and said very little all the way home.

I slept like a log that night and then suddenly it was Monday morning again and back to work.

My work colleagues all asked about how my trip was, what the others were like, the lads enquiring "did I pull", "any hookers", "how was the weed" and so on. I didn't admit to anyone that the truth was I couldn't actually remember anything and so just palmed off the questions with standard replies, "yes it was a great laugh", "had a brilliant time", "we all got on really well", "such a great place", "yes lots of weed, the red-light district, some sightseeing", etc.

As the week progressed a few internal emails were doing the rounds from Vanessa, Tom and co. They were all pressing me to see if I had remembered anything yet, asking what really happened and such like. I had given my mobile number to Vanessa and she had texted me quite a few times. I wanted to arrange to meet her but didn't seem to find the courage, I was still really embarrassed and confused. In honesty it was completely occupying my mind, and I was finding it hard to concentrate at work. I had played all sorts of weird scenarios back to myself, like been date raped, kidnapped or some other such ridiculous stuff. All the following weekend my mind was playing tricks on me and I couldn't get it out of my head.

On Sunday evening I made a decision. I was going to go back to Amsterdam and try to re-trace my steps. I logged into my airmiles account, I knew I had built up loads of flight time with all the other destinations I had been to, and I also knew that you could use airmiles to book hotels as well.

On Monday morning I asked my boss first thing if I could have Friday off again, making some excuse about a family gathering. He was a good boss and had no problem with that, besides I still had some holiday days to use up. I had already booked flights and the hotel before the end of the day, the exact same flights and hotel that we had booked the weekend before.

Back to the Dam

So, I had formulated a brief plan. I was going to check into the Marriott and chill there for a bit and then head back to The Grasshopper.

I didn't want to get there too early as, knowing myself well, I would only be tempted to indulge in the pleasures of Amsterdam again. I was determined to stay off the weed and just allow myself a few beers, thus keeping a clear head and hopefully being able to attempt to retrace my steps and come up with some answers as to what on earth happened to me the fortnight before.

After relaxing in my hotel room, having grabbed forty winks and some food on room service, I decided on heading back to the Grasshopper at around 7pm. The others said that they had lost track of me somewhere around 9-10pm.

It was busy by the time I arrived and I went to the bar to order a beer. The same big hairy guy was serving.

"Oh, hey man, back so soon?"

"Yep, couldn't stay away" I smiled back at him. "Actually, do you have a quick minute, I need to ask you something"?"

"Sure man, shoot"

I quickly explained to him about my total memory loss and how it had been really bothering me.

"I don't suppose you noticed anything?"

The big bar man was laughing hard at me. "For real? Wow man that's funny"

"Glad you find it so amusing mate" I snapped back at him.

"Sorry dude I can't really help. You and your mates were totally out of it, but you were all having a great time and weren't causing any trouble or anything so we kept on serving you. I did notice you were on the balcony outside at one point, talking to some guy. I think you left with him but I couldn't tell you anything else man"

"Oh, ok. So you didn't recognise this other guy?"

"Well yer sort of, he comes in here from time to time but I'm sorry man I don't know his name or anything. Just let me ask Jacco, see if he knows him"

Jacco apparently was the other huge hairy guy who sold the joints from the desk next to the bar. Jacco came over and I explained the same story again. He just shrugged his shoulders and said..

"No dude, don't know the other guy. Anyway you want a spliff man? On the house."

"That's really kind, but I staying off it this weekend mate. Thanks anyway"

I stood at the bar, slowly drinking my first beer, watching the bar man work his magic when pouring the frothy beers. I ordered another and then headed out to the balcony area and sat outside, lighting a smoke. Nothing at all was coming back to me. I was disappointed, hoping all the while that something would jog my memory bank and all would be revealed.

Finishing off my second beer I decided to head off to the red-light district. I knew vaguely which direction it was, but took my time and allowed the sights not to pass me by. It was so busy with tourists mainly, but there also seemed to be a lot of Dutch and German people as well. I ambled around the district, window shopping and looking with fascination at all that was on offer.

If you haven't been into the red-light zone in Amsterdam, you should. It's basically rows and rows of narrow streets with "ladies of the night" standing in "shop" windows, offering their sexual services. I think this place could cater for all tastes. The ladies were all shapes and sizes, all colours and nationalities, trannies, trans-sexuals, from seriously beautiful to seriously ugly. Lots of them were stood in doorways, trying to get punters in through their doors. It wasn't my bag at all, but nonetheless it was still fascinating just wondering around and taking in the whole atmosphere. I began to wonder why the better-looking girls would need to sell themselves for money, but then I supposed it allowed you an affluent lifestyle and was deemed fairly safe as it was all within a controlled environment.

After about half an hour I stopped at a food joint and got myself a large portion of Bitterballen. I was munching them outside and was beginning to think about giving up and to go and find a "café" for another beer and perhaps a spliff. Just one won't harm I though.

"Jonesy. Jonesy. Is that you?" someone was shouting. This guy came rushing up to me, grabbed me in a bear hug, and said "It is you! Wow I didn't think I would see you again. What the hell are you doing here?"

The guy pulled away from the bear hug and looked at me. I looked back at him, and had no recognition of who this person was. He could obviously tell from the blank look on my face.

"It's me, Fritz! Jonesy how are you?"

"Oh, hi, I'm good thanks" I hesitated.

"Are you ok dude, you're looking a bit lost. Too many spliffs again?" he laughed.

"No, no, just a couple of beers. Err sorry to ask but how do you know me?"

He looked at me like I had just stabbed him in the heart. "What do you mean, you must remember me from two weeks ago dude? We had a mad weekend...."

It seemed this fella knew my name and who I was, so I made my confession. "I honestly don't really remember anything from that weekend. I hope you can help me with that? What's your name again?"

"Fritz" he exclaimed. "Are you serious dude, you don't remember me?"

"Nope, not at all"

He looked at me again, this time with a less hurtful look and said "Jesus dude, well we did get crazy high and drunk. I tell you what, let's just go for a beer and I will tell you everything" he laughed again.

"Well I was just about to go and find a café, is there one near here?"

"Follow me Jonesy!"

I needed to take a chance; he looked harmless enough and so I followed beside him and he ducked into a side street which led down to one of the many canals, where a café stood with some tables and chairs outside, all occupied by people enjoying themselves, smoking, drinking and chatting away. Inside Fritz found a small table and he sat down, pulling up a chair for me. He waved over the barman who obviously knew him, and then came back in a couple of minutes with two beers. In the meanwhile I was looking at this Fritz character. He was around his mid 30's I guessed but looked older, was only about 5ft 7 and had weathered skin and eyes that almost disappeared into his head. His stained teeth needed a dentist badly. They were dark brown and crooked, with a few missing. Not really a typical Dutch looking person at all, but he clearly was as he spoke the lingo.

He turned to look at me and raised his pint glass. We chinked and drank a big slug each. Then he said

"So dude, you don't remember anything? Wow that's freaky man"

I explained the story to him, about waking up on Sunday morning with total memory loss. I told him it had also "freaked" me out and that's why I came back again. I wanted to retrace my steps and find out what on earth happened those two missing days. I explained I knew that I wasn't in the hotel at all on Saturday as my colleagues had been looking for me. Fritz took another gulp of beer and then lit up a huge spliff that he had been rolling while I talked. He offered me a drag. I shook my head, telling him I wanted to keep a grip on reality and find out what happened during all those missing hours of my life.

Fritz looked amazed and was laughing a lot at my expense.

"Jesus dude, far out!! I met you at The Grasshopper and we spent the weekend together, we got on so well and it seemed you were up for a good time man. So I kind of took you under my arm and we hit it hard man! Don't you remember coming to Kampen with me? That's where I live dude?"

I looked at him blankly and simply shrugged "I swear the last thing I remember was being in The Grasshopper with my friends and then being woken up on Sunday morning in the hotel. That's it"

"Jesus dude, far out" he said again. "Are you here for the whole weekend?"

"Yep"

"Then I better help you out man. Come on let's get another beer and then we will go. I don't have any plans really dude, so I'm going take you on the same path we took the other week. Fuck this is crazy dude"

"Err, sure, go where"

"Kampen man, Kampen. You can stay at mine again dude, no problem"

We chatted more, finished our beers and headed towards the train station, stopping quickly at my hotel so I could grab my bag. Apparently, we got the exact same train at 10.38pm to Kampen, wherever that was. On arriving about an hour and a half later, Fritz and I had become well acquainted (again) and he had picked up some tins of beer at the station. He had rung ahead on his mobile, it seemed to his flat mates, and had been laughing his head off during the call and looking at me. He repeated my name several times during the call. He must have been explaining the situation (in Dutch) to his pals and seemed excited by their responses.

Throughout the journey I was thinking to myself how could I possibly have no recollection of a train journey, especially as it was not a short one.

"Dude this is going be a blast again! Are you ready for this Jonesy?!"

"Honestly, not really! I hope I don't disappoint."

Fritz's pad was only a couple of minutes' walk from Kampen station. He walked quickly as he still seemed really exhilarated. Putting the key in a ground level door, there were a few steps straight up to what must be a flat. He shouted ahead

"Jonesy's here!!"

Fritz's Mates

I climbed the stairs behind Fritz and we came to another door which had been left open. I was feeling very apprehensive now and wondering if I had really lost my mind. What the hell was I doing? I didn't know what I was letting myself in for. This really was either crazy or just plain stupid.

The flat was bigger than I imagined. There was a big lounge area with an open plan kitchen, and several rooms off the lounge, presumably bedrooms and bathrooms.

Seating in the smoky lounge were two other people. One girl and another guy.

"Well, I better introduce you again Jonesy" Fritz laughed. "This is Mila and this is Daan". They both stood up to greet me.

Daan was what I might call a typical Dutch guy. Tall, blonde and good looking. I held out my hand to shake his outstretched one. He firmly shook it and beamed at me broadly.

Then I turned to Mila and I swear I think my heart actually stopped. I think that too, my jaw had literally dropped to the floor. Mila was absolutely beautiful. No, that was an understatement. She was stunning, like something straight off the catwalk or a movie set. I swallowed hard and tried to gather myself, holding out my hand to sake her's. But she ignored my hand and pulled me right into her, giving me a great big hug. I could feel her large and extremely firm breasts push into my chest, and she kissed each of my reddening cheeks in turn.

After she pulled away, I simply starred at her. Her gorgeous bright blue eyes were almost level with mine and I'm 6ft 3. She was just wearing jeans and a white t-shirt that emphasized her large chest. Long blond hair that fell onto and beyond her shoulders. Her blue jeans seemed like they were climbing her long legs, clinging tightly to her thighs, showing every lovely curve and as she turned to sit down the jeans didn't hide her perfectly formed behind. I became aware that I was standing on the spot, still starring at her in wonder and disbelief. I snapped myself out of it and Fritz offered me to sit down on a sofa opposite the other two, another beer being pushed into my hand by him.

Daan and Mila were both looking at me like I should have something to say. I gathered myself and again began to repeat my story of what I knew of the weekend before last. While speaking they were both staring at me in disbelief. I was thinking whilst telling them everything that I knew that I was beginning to get a little tried to repeating my story. I decided that if I meet anyone else this weekend that I "knew" I would simply pretend to recognise them. The questions came from them all as I spoke, more laughing and joking at my expense. It was understandable.

"Verdomde hel" said Mila. This was actually the only Dutch I knew, "Fucking hell" she had declared loudly. Mila was rolling up a fat cone, sparked it up and handed it to me. I knew I had promised myself not to smoke the green stuff this weekend, but circumstances had changed I thought to myself. Besides, how could I possibly refuse this amazing creature? I inhaled deeply and soon began to feel the mild effects, and my confidence began to grow a little.

"Let's go to the café" Daan suggested.

It was now almost 1am. They all jumped up and we headed out. The café it turned out was directly beneath the flat. Convenient I thought. We talked and laughed, I kept the weed to just an occasional drag and a few more beers were drunk. The café was beginning to close up, it was 2am now and so we all headed back upstairs to freshen up and get changed. Fritz had made a plan which was more or less to recreate my last trip to Kampen, and they all gladly agreed.

As it turned out, the fortnight before, the four of us, myself, Fritz, Daan and Mila had stayed up the whole Friday night in the café, then went to some nightclub and continued back at the flat, drinking and smoking the green, carrying on all night and all through the Saturday daytime right up until Fritz had put me back on the last train to Amsterdam, to ensure I wouldn't miss my flight home on Sunday morning.

I was beginning to understand why I had total memory loss.

The Nightclub

It was now about 2.45am, the club again was only a short walk away from the flat. It was apparently open until 6am every Friday and Saturday night.

I was feeling great by now. I understood what had happened to me and although I could never fill in the fine details, at least I knew that I had been safe and not part of some gang bang or anything weird like that. A wave of relief had come over me and given me an added energy. My head felt clear, despite all the beers, and my mind was at rest. I was so pleased that I had by chance bumped in Fritz again and that I had returned to Amsterdam (and Kampen). Now I was in a real party mood again.

We didn't have to que; Fritz was waved through with us by one of the bouncers. Fritz smiled at me and whispered "I get him his snow supplies, not everyone in Holland just smokes cannabis you know" he winked at me.

The nightclub was absolutely incredible. It didn't look much from the outside and I was thinking it might be a small place, but cramped to the rafters going by the number of people still queuing to get in. It was the opposite. It was on three floors and had a total of four different dance floors, each with its own bar and each playing a different genre of music. It was an amazing place. One room was playing general pop, another techno music, one seemed to focus more on heavy metal/rock and the final room was oddly one of these silent discos where people wore head phones that played some kind of chill-out music. I think this was more for people who chose to partake in ecstasy. It seemed my new pals preferred the techno scene. That was fine with me.

We found some spare seats, more like sofas, and Daan headed to the bar. I just sat and watched the dance floor for a while. People were gyrating, bouncing up and down, dipping their shoulders and swaying their hips. Some of the dancers were really impressive and moving their lower bodies in time to the beat pattern. I was very much a "dad" dancer and hoped that I could escape the dance floor.

We shouted to each other over the music, Fritz sat next to me and the others on a sofa opposite. Then Daan and Fritz got up to dance. Shit, I thought, please don't drag me up there. Mila jumped up and parked herself next to me. It was impossible to avoid body contact on the small sofa, and I could feel Mila's warm body next to mine.

"Wow, what a cool place" I shouted at her. She leaned in and spoke into my ear, her breath tickling my neck.

"So you still don't remember this place"

"No not at all, weird hey?"

She laughed at me and smiled. Wow what a smile, I think I was in love.

"Come on, show me some of those great moves to yours" She grabbed my hand and pulled me up towards where Daan and Fritz were jigging about. I had no choice, but with the beers I was feeling loose and mildly confident that I could get away with not making a complete fool of myself. Mila began gyrating against me, dancing up really close and in the sexiest way I could have imagined. Her movements were incredible, and soon she became surrounded by other men who wanted to chance their luck. I really couldn't blame them. However, she ignored their attention and continued to focus on me. I couldn't help it, my senses overtook any control my mind might have over them and I found myself getting aroused again, just as I had with Vanessa. It must have been the effects of the weed, they say it makes sex more pleasurable. Mila knew it, and she loved it, dancing ever more closely to me, her hands sometimes brushing against my erection. I danced with her, trying my best to keep up with her movements. She was laughing all the while and her eyes were totally focused on mine. I'm in heaven I thought to myself and I lost all inhibitions and pressed my hardness into her body as we danced.

Surely there was no way on earth I had slept with this perfect creature last time me met. I refused to believe that I wouldn't remember that. The truth was she was no doubt the most beautiful woman I had ever met.

After another track we all headed back to our sofas. I pulled my shirt out of my jeans to cover my groin until I had calmed down, I didn't want the others to see how helplessly under Mila's spell I was.

The evening continued and went by in a flash, and soon it was kicking out time. I was wondering what would happen now.

Back at the flat Fritz decided it was time for another spliff and a beer. Fritz obviously lived off cannabis, and he barely had a moment where he wasn't either smoking one or rolling one.

Mila sat next to me, and her hand was on my knee as we spoke.

Was this really going to happen? Did this breathtaking and exquisite woman want me?

After a while Daan announced he was going to go and crash out. Fritz rolled another large one and said he was going to listen to some music in his room and call it a night. I was left alone with Mila.

"Well I guess I should go and crash out too. I don't suppose you want to join me?" I chanced my luck. She looked across at me and smiled.

"I'm flattered Jonesy but I actually have a girlfriend. You tried to get me to your bed last time, but I guess you don't remember. It's ok though, I get it. You're such a great guy and if I were not gay then I would say "yes", so please don't be offended"

I looked at her, pretending, "Oh thank god!!" I lied to her "I would have been totally mortified if we had slept together and I hadn't remembered. How offensive would that have been?!! You really are incredibly beautiful woman."

She kissed the top of my forehead and stood up. "Thank you Jonesy. I will see you later and I can show you around our town. Right now, I need some sleep"

"I'd really like that, goodnight lovely"

I can't say I wasn't a little disappointed, but nor was I surprised to be politely turned down by Mila.

I think I must have fallen asleep instantly, and woke around 1pm on Saturday lunchtime.

Kampen

When I woke, I actually felt really fresh. No-one else seemed to be up yet so I clicked on the kettle and took the opportunity to have a shower.

After drying and changing I headed back to the kitchen. Mila was up and about.

"Morning Jonesy" she handed me a hot coffee and kissed my check.

"Morning lovely, thanks"

"So I promised you a guided tour. What time do you have to get back to Amsterdam?"

"Any time really, so long as I'm back in time to catch my plane"

"Ok, cool. Kampen has lots to see so I will make sure you're in plenty of time to get the train back tonight. Do you have plans to go out tonight or anything"

"No to be honest, I think I will just chill in the hotel bar and get a good night's sleep. There's nothing worse that traveling with a bad hangover!"

"Agreed" she smiled. "I don't think Daan or Fritz will be up for a few hours yet so it's good to have some company for the day"

"So where's your girlfriend? Does she live in Kampen"

"She does but she's away right now, in England actually. She is visiting her brother for a few weeks. I'm really missing her"

"Ahh, well I'm sure she's missing you too"

After a couple more coffees Mila said we should get something to eat in the café downstairs, they do a great breakfast, and then she would show me around.

Kampen is a really really lovely place as it turned out. It sits on the river Ijssel and has a beautifully preserved old town, with numerous churches and historical buildings and the ancient city wall still remains in some parts. It also has an old wind mill that dates back to the 1840's.

Mila was an excellent guide and very knowledgeable. She explained about the history of the town, dating back to the Middle Ages when the town grew as it was well placed to have a busy trade route with the Baltic and how it soon established itself as a prosperous leading city in northern Europe. It had been involved in numerous wars over the centuries but trade had begun to fall as the river had problems with silting up and becoming too shallow for trade ships. Attempts had been made over the years to dredged the river only for it to silt up again. As a result, the town had several delta-like mouths.

It had been home to many famous artists, poets, acters, musicians, war heroes, radicles and sports stars.

She took me to The Stedelijk Museum, showed me the famous city gates which still stood with parts of the old city wall, an incredible gothic church (St Nicholas) and we crossed one of the three bridges (The Stadsbrug). We had a late lunch at fabulous seafood restaurant on the river and I can honestly say I had one of the best days of my life and in the company of a truly wonderful person, that I was totally and completely in love with by the end of the day. She was so kind and thoughtful and also was so funny and clever. She was simply perfect in every way.

We eventually got back to the flat, stopping again at the café beneath for a quick beer at around 6pm. I had insisted on buying her lunch and drinks for being so kind to me, despite my small budget.

Fritz was smoking a fat one on the sofa, of course, there was no sign of Daan.

"Jonesy! Good day dude?"

"Totally fantastic cheers Fritz, Mila has been amazing, showing be your lovely town. I've had such a great day" I said, giving Mila a warm hug. "But sadly, I've run out of time and should be getting a train back to Amsterdam"

"Oh, ok dude. I will walk you there if you like"

"No, it's ok" (I wasn't good at goodbyes) "I know the way". I collected my bits and pieces, exchanged numbers with them both, gave hugs, thanks and farewells and insisted that they should look me up if they were ever in England.

Back to Reality

Sunday morning, the flight and underground back home went in no time at all. I had slept much of the journey.

I got back to the house where I was living at the time in Islington. My house mates were lounging about, watching some movie and just chilling before Monday morning came.

I chucked my bag down on the floor and flopped on the sofa, recounting the story of my weekend. I reached into my coat pocket for my cigarettes and found the large cone Fritz had rolled me earlier.

"Anyone fancy a bedtime spliff" I asked my housemates. They all nodded and we passed it round.

Monday came. I arranged to meet Vanessa, Steve and Tom (Charlotte had declined) on Wednesday evening at the Punch & Judy in Covent Garden and again repeated my findings to them. They were all dying to know. Vanessa was staring, open mouthed, as I told the story with as much information as I could, but without over stating the beauty of Mila as I was still hoping for a night of passion with Vanessa, and obviously didn't want her to think Mila was something special.

As it turned out Vanessa and I did hook up a few times and we enjoyed each other's company and bodies. It was never going to more than that however, as neither of us wanted anything serious.

And so, life moved on, and after two or three more years I left London (having become a bit sick of it) and returned to my hometown in Cheshire.

I don't want to end on a negative, but I do find it odd really, how people come into your life and then evaporate just as quickly. How experiences, whatever they may be (nights out, weekends away, holidays, places you live, jobs you had, sexual partners, people you meet along the way) just become memories in no time at all. Yes, I still have a hardcore of friends that I have known for years and years, but these people have been, other than family, the only real constants in my life.

Whilst writing this it has made me wonder how Mila and indeed Vanessa are, what have they been doing, are they married, do they have kids, are they happy. I also looked through my mobile and found I still had Fritz's number programmed into the memory. I sent a text but it came back undelivered. I seriously doubt that he is still alive, he looked half dead when I met him! Perhaps he is still going and is stoned in some café somewhere in Holland, who knows?

I wonder often what is the actual point of humanity, of being alive for the short time that we get. Is there a purpose to it all? Is there really "a meaning of life"? Well, I have never come up with the answers to that, and I don't suppose any of us really do?

I will simply end with saying to my readers, all I know is that you have to make the best of it for whatever time you are given. I hope you find joy in the pursuit of happiness and this little story has in a small way added to that and put a smile on your face.

THE END